FOREWORD

It gives me great pleasure to see Welsh farming life – and special Welsh breeds – being celebrated in this booklet. In my work for television I meet many remarkable and dedicated farming families, who are passionate about the animals they breed. Steve Dubé pays tribute to a number of breeders in this book, and it reminds me of the commitment, enthusiasm and hard work that I have seen in so many others who have appeared on *Cefn Gwlad* over the years. I am sure that readers will be delighted to discover that there are special Welsh breeds for many farm animals – not just the famous Welsh Black or the Welsh Cob but Welsh Harlequin Ducks, several breeds of sheep – not forgetting, of course, the very lovable Welsh pig!

Visitors to Wales almost invariably praise the landscape, and rightly so. But this booklet will no doubt prompt admiration too for the people who work the land and lovingly raise their animals on it. This is all part of the rich pattern of country life as we know it in Wales – long may it continue.

Dai Jones, Llanilar

INTRODUCTION

Pontrhydfendigaid Fair.   Photo. by D. J. Davies, Lampeter.

Welsh farmers are proud of their animals. It's a sentiment that makes the Royal Welsh Show the largest agricultural event in Europe, reflecting the rural nature of a green and pleasant land. And farming certainly plays an important role in the country's economy: the latest census figures show 21,839 full time and 22,331 part-time farmers, with another 13,295 farm workers. This total of 57,465 is around 2% of the working population in what was, don't forget, Europe's first industrial country.

The last century saw a dramatic exodus from the land, with farms growing larger and more mechanised. The tractor, four-by-four and the all-terrain quad bike completely replaced the horse in little more than 70 years as the industrial revolution completed its transformation of the countryside and the farm subsidy system encouraged intensive methods of food production.

But a new revolution has now begun, with subsidies no longer linked to output and agri-environment projects encouraging wildlife-friendly systems. Consumer demand has increased the possibilities for organic and specialist produce, often using indigenous breeds of livestock that had been reduced to rare-breed status by the fashion for fast-growing, high-yielding types imported from abroad.

Before the arrival of cheap transport made possible the use of non-native breeds, farmers everywhere developed their own varieties of livestock and shaped their agriculture in distinctive ways. In Wales, specific breeds were developed to suit local climate and topography. Some of these breeds, and the people who look after them, will be found in these pages.

Many of the stories have deep roots. Nearly all our farm animals and tools were known to ancient human beings. By the time Neolithic peoples arrived in Britain around 2500 BC, cattle, sheep and pigs had already been domesticated at least 3,000 years earlier in the region of the Middle East now known as Iraq.

The newcomers to these islands probably brought cattle, sheep, goats and pigs with them, but at least two species of wild cattle are thought to be indigenous to Britain – the aurochs or *Bos*

Celtic coin, featuring a pony.

primigenius and the 'Celtic' shorthorn – *Bos longifrons*. The auroch is thought to be the ancestor of picturesque breeds like the Highland and the Longhorn, both of which can be seen on modern Welsh farms. The shorthorn gave us the oldest Welsh breeds – the White Park and Welsh Black, although the auroch too is thought to be an ancestor of the White Park. These striking cattle can be seen grazing the National Trust's landscaped Dinefwr Park in Llandeilo, where a herd has lived almost continuously for more than a thousand years. The famous Welsh Black may be a descendant of the cattle brought from the continent by a new wave of Bronze Age immigrants around 1500 BC.

These two breeds were the kind of cattle that the Romans would have found when they arrived in Britain, and it is only in more recent times that continental breeds like the black-and-white dairy cows, the Holstein Friesians, and the thick-set Charolais beef cattle have been seen on Welsh farms.

The Romans would also have noticed the Celtic pony. Archaeologists have found parts of harnesses and chariots dating back to the Bronze Age, and Julius Caesar was so impressed with the speed of the chariot ponies that he took some back with him to Rome. Cattle, ponies and pigs were of great importance to the British, and appear frequently in the earliest recorded stories. Ponies are depicted on many Celtic coins.

Sheep were among the first animals to be domesticated as early as 7,000 years ago, and were probably brought to Britain by Neolithic people. The nearest type to these ancient sheep is the Soay, a small brown animal with long curved horns and a tendency to shed its fleece every year. The Romans brought a much superior beast with a white face and a finer fleece and the Welsh Mountain is thought to be a cross of the two types. But it was the monks of medieval Britain who really developed sheep farming. For them – and up to recent times – the animal was valued not as a provider of meat but as a source of milk and wool. Serious efforts to exploit the potential for meat

only began as recently as the Industrial Revolution of the eighteenth century when the population expanded rapidly. Today more than 40 breeds are exhibited every year at the Royal Welsh Show. In 2007 there were 4,500,000 breeding ewes in Wales, compared with just under three million people.

Every sheep farmer needs a dog, and in Wales it is often the Border Collie. But a specific Welsh breed of sheepdog was formally recognised in 1997, bred over the centuries to bring in sheep from the mountains, even on its own. The drovers who once took huge herds of livestock to markets in England bred the Corgi, while hunt enthusiasts developed terriers to help them flush out their prey.

WELSH CORGI

Cattle and sheep are still the mainstays of modern farming while the pig, once commonplace in terraced yards as well as in farm pigsties, has become something of a rarity, restricted to enthusiastic smallholders with rare breeds, who often deal directly with specialist butchers or sell direct through farmers' markets. The only native breed, the Welsh Pig, can be seen in its traditional surroundings at the National Trust's Llanerchaeron estate near Aberaeron.

Poultry was once found in every farmyard, and was traditionally the woman's domain – a way of earning a few pennies by selling eggs and table birds to supplement the main enterprise. Specific Welsh breeds of poultry were standardised by enthusiasts in the twentieth century from types that were common in the Welsh countryside, although no one has yet given us a Welsh chicken!

WELSH BLACKS

Above: Ffion – already adept at handling calves.
Below: the stunning view from Talymignedd Isaf.

There was never really any alternative to Welsh Black cattle for farmers Arwel and Sioned Jones of Talymignedd Isaf, near Nantlle, in the Snowdonia National Park.

Arwel's father, Hugh Arfon Jones, who is still active in the 1,600-acre family partnership (100 acres is rented), inherited the Mignedd herd of Welsh Blacks from his own father, William John Jones, who first registered the herd as pedigree in 1953.

Arwel is the sixth generation of his family to farm Welsh Black cattle, so they were a prized family tradition – and it was the same for Sioned. It was her grandfather, Emwnt Richards, an estate farm-worker, who first registered her family's herd of Welsh Blacks, called Carnedd Dafydd, after the name of the mountain that overlooked his home in Capel Curig, in 1972.

The Welsh Black tradition stayed over a family move to Denbighshire and accompanied Sioned's mother Catrin and her husband Robert Jones when they moved after their marriage to a farm on the Llŷn peninsula.

'I got interested when I was little,' says Sioned, who has her hands full these days looking after the couple's four children – Elin aged 14, Tomos 10, Ffion 6 and Robat aged one – but finds time to serve on the council of the Welsh Black Cattle Society like her father before her.

'My parents would go around the shows and I just wanted to carry on, really. I'm looking forward to doing the shows again when the children are older.'

Sionel and Arwel now run 50 Welsh Black breeding cows with followers and two bulls. Ysguboriau Bleddyn 40th is in his fourth year at Talymignedd and will be leaving soon for pastures new. His replacement is Nantrhys Sambo 2nd, bought last year from the well-known farmer, television presenter and singer, Dai Jones, Llanilar.

Welsh Black may be an obsession the couple inherited from both sides of the family, but they admire the breed in its own right. These animals excel both as pure-breds and as dams for cross-bred beef animals.

'They are good mothers and very good milkers and we keep them until they are eight or nine years old. They don't use as much feed compared with cross-bred or continental cattle, they look after themselves and are very hardy as well as being very quiet cattle,' asserts Sioned.

Welsh folklore tells us of many types of cattle. There were the gigantic long-horned oxen in the Mabinogion tale of Culhwch and Olwen – perhaps a folk memory of the wild auroch that was the ancestor of all modern cattle.

But the medieval poets most often mentioned black as the colour of the much favoured bulls. Market records from North Pembrokeshire at the turn of the 16th century show that nearly 60% of the cattle were black, 13% brown and nearly 10% speckled.

And by the time the drovers got involved in establishing the first banks in order to secure the transport of money as well as farm animals between Wales and England, it was the Black Ox that gave its name to the bank established at the droving town of Llandovery. By that time it had earned its description as 'the black gold from the Welsh hills'.

'We don't buy in so we put the best cows to the bull and cross some of the others with a Charolais bull to rear as store cattle. We sell stores at Bryncir market, while we sell pure-breds at Dolgellau,' says Sioned. 'We used to fatten all the cattle but we are getting more now by selling them as stores.'

They are fond of the meat, which they say is different from that of the fast-growing continental. The animal needs to be mature – the legal age limit for slaughter is currently 30 months or under – and the meat should be hung to mature and tenderise, ideally for one month.

'It's lovely meat and very tender and they are starting to sell it in the market now because a lot of the guest houses up here put it on the menu. People are asking for it now and want to know where it comes from.'

And the couple say the prejudice against the Welsh Black as a smaller beast is disappearing. Where once a Welsh Black store animal could be £200 cheaper than a Charolais of the same age, the Welsh Black now fetches the same kind of money.

'We hope farmers do go back to the Welsh Black because this is a traditional native breed and it's nice to keep the old-fashioned breeds. We've seen a lot of cattle imported from abroad bringing in disease with them, so there would be less of that, and these cattle are hardier and more adapted to our climate.'

Before the family joined the Tir Gofal agri-environment scheme, their cattle wintered outside and would thrive despite the harsh weather and rough pasture. Now they are housed during the winter months in order to minimise damage to the land. This attention to the natural environment earned the couple the Royal Welsh Show's prestigious £1,000 Agri-environment Award in 2003. It was a reward for improving biodiversity on the picturesque farm – work that included a new cattle shed and an under-floor slurry store to prevent possible pollution in rainy weather, extensive double fencing and hedging and a range of other improvements.

The Jones family has been part of a twentieth-century revival that has seen great advances in Welsh Black breeding, and the two distinct strains of the stocky north Wales beef type and the more dairy-like south Wales or Castlemartin beast have produced an animal that combines beefiness with ease of calving and the milking ability that gives strong growing calves. Dairy farmers are also finding that the Welsh Black is an excellent dairy-beef cross, especially on heifers.

And this is a genuine British breed, developed in Britain solely from British Welsh Black genetics with no input from imported Welsh Black bloodlines or other breeds. That makes it ideally suited to British conditions, where it performs well in a variety of situations, including lowland beef breeding and finishing systems. But its reputation is built on the breed's ability to thrive on the rough grazing of marginal and upland areas, where its hardiness and active foraging habit, ease of calving, and mothering ability, outscores its continental competitors.

The meat itself is considered second to none. A blind tasting by 12 top chefs in in London's *La Chaumière* Restaurant in June 2003 concluded that a fillet steak of organic Welsh Black beef from John James's farm at Tŷ Llwyd, Felingwm near Carmarthen was the best in texture, colour, tenderness and flavour compared to the same cut from eight other continental or British breeds.

At a time when farming commentators are predicting a future in a more crowded world where meat is reared solely on upland grass with the lower land reserved for food and energy crops, the Welsh Black is the kind of breed that will answer the need.

At award-winning restaurant Y Polyn in Carmarthenshire, the chefs swear by Welsh Black beef.

John James, Tŷ Llwyd.

The actual origins of the Welsh Black are unknown. Forerunners of the breed certainly existed in Roman times, and some commentators believe it is based on cattle from the Iberian Peninsula.

The modern breed is a combination of two types – one a dairy and one a beef breed. Farmers with the milky South Wales or Castlemartin Black made the first effort to form a society to improve the breed in 1867 and the first breed pedigree register, with details of 96 dual-purpose cows and 56 bulls, was published in 1874. The first register of the stocky North Wales or Anglesey type followed nearly ten years later in 1883.

The two types were amalgamated into a common register in 1905 after a meeting of the two societies in the Boar's Head, Carmarthen agreed to form a single society. The main gathering of breeders since 1957 has been at Dolgellau, where there are now four annual sales of pedigree Welsh Blacks. There are two others at Llandovery and one each at Abergavenny and Carlisle every year.

WHITE PARK CATTLE

Former dairy farmer Wyn Davies has learned to proceed with caution when one of the 28 White Park cows at Dinefwr Park, Llandeilo, has calved.

Wyn, now a warden at the National Trust country park, looks after the oldest herd of Britain's most ancient breed, and says he has to make sure he ear-tags the calves, as required by law, within the first twelve hours of life or he'll never get near them.

'You have to be very careful because they are very protective of their young and the mother could go for you. They are very flighty and very fast on their feet, and they are not the easiest to handle,' he says. They also have large horns that they are able to use effectively if they feel under threat.

Wyn believes their skittishness and protective instincts could stem from a close relationship to the auroch, the ancient wild ancestor of all cattle breeds, and their primitive instincts can be seen by the thousands of people who visit the park every year.

'The whole herd will join in to protect individuals. During the summer the adult herd will be off grazing somewhere while the young calves stay behind in a group to bask in the sun, and one

cow will stay behind to look after them,' he says.

They also have an uncanny sixth sense, particularly for weather. On a sunny day they can sometimes be seen disappearing to shelter, and sure enough, there will be a storm that night. 'Because of their ancestry they have held onto these primitive instincts that modern cattle have lost,' says Wyn.

The herd of 28 cows, ten followers or younger cattle with current bull Hembury Merlin, is one of the largest in a total of just over 100 herds worldwide and is the only one that has roamed the same pastures since before the Norman Conquest.

'These cattle have always been here. This is their ancestral home,' says Wyn of the 800 acres of eighteenth-century landscaped park around a twelfth-century castle that was once the royal court of the Princes of the medieval south Wales kingdom of Deheubarth.

'If you took the White Park cattle out of Dinefwr it would be like taking the lions out of Longleat or the ravens from the Tower of London.'

These days the cattle at Dinefwr have a dual purpose. The parkland is a Site of Special Scientific Interest where the poor-quality grassland is home to over 160 varieties of lichen and is a breeding ground for the rare redstart. Cattle help to maintain the pasture, but modern breeds would be unable to prosper.

'They do well on very poor grazing so we use them as a tool to manage the pastures,' says Wyn. 'And there's a ready market for breeding heifers. One that's ready for the bull or has already been served will fetch up to £1,000. There's also a market for the meat, which is top quality, and we could market our own, but we have not gone into that because we have not got the capacity or the manpower.'

Membury Merlin, the current daddy of the herd, will leave the park in 2010 to be swapped with another bull from a different herd in order to avoid inbreeding. A swap takes place every three years, when the bull's daughters are ready for mating.

White Park cattle, historically known as Park, White Forest, White Horned or Wild White, are the direct descendants of those that were here when the Romans arrived 2,000 years ago. Roman

White Park cattle have been used for many purposes during their long history. Apart from their use as a form of currency, they are thought to have been special sacrificial animals to the mystic Celtic priesthood of Druids. They were used as draft animals in the nineteenth century. When the last plough ox in the Dinefwr herd was slaughtered in 1871 at the age of fourteen, he weighed 23 hundredweight (about 1,170 kilograms) and had horns five feet long from tip to tip (that's about one and a half metres long). Some herds were milked in the early twentieth century but the commercial value of the breed now lies in its beef qualities and its use as a crossing sire. Results from several commercial herds show that White Park bulls cause scarcely any problems when used as a crossing sire, and the cross-bred calves are notably active at birth.

writers refer to white cattle being specially selected for Druidic rites.

The herd at Dinefwr Park, Llandeilo has grazed the fields around the former Welsh royal castle – apart from a break of 16 years in the late twentieth century – at least since the tenth century when Hywel Dda, King of Wales held court there. Oral tradition states that Hywel brought together a council of noblemen from across Wales to establish the first all-Wales legal code, and the Laws, which survive in written form from the thirteenth century, state that this special breed of cattle, completely white except for black markings on their noses, ears, tails and feet, were used as a sort of currency and as tribute and fines paid to Welsh princes.

In 1210 the wife of William de Breos, the Norman Lord of Brecon, tried unsuccessfully to appease King John with a gift of a White Park bull and four hundred cows.

Several herds were emparked in various parklands in Britain in the thirteenth, fourteenth and fifteenth centuries and there were more than a dozen pure White Park herds in the early 1900s. The number had halved by the turn of the twentieth century when the breed registration programme began, but numbers dwindled during the Second World War to fewer than 100 registered females in just four herds – the Dinefwr, Cadzow, Woburn and Whipsnade herds. With the country threatened by invasion, the government considered the breed important enough for a small unit to be shipped to the United States for safe keeping. When the Rare Breeds Survival Trust was formed in 1973 the four remaining herds were given the communal name White Park.

The White Park is a large breed, with cows weighing on average from twelve to twelve and a half hundredweight – around 600kg. Its long hindquarters favour ease of calving, as well as beef production.

The cattle are white with colour on the ears, nose, teats and feet and around the rims of their eyes. The intensity of these markings varies from herd to herd.

White cattle with such coloured points are first mentioned in old Irish sagas dating back almost 2,000 years. The early nineteenth century authority John Storer believed they were the direct descendants of the Wild White Bull that roamed the forests which once covered the British Isles.

Outside Britain, there are herds in the United States, Germany, Denmark, Australia and Canada but the status of the breed is listed as critical, with a worldwide population of approximately 500 purebred females in 79 herds, plus bulls and young stock. The breeds that appear to be most closely related to the White Park are the Highland and Galloway of Scotland.

Brindled cow, white speckled,
Spotted cow, bold freckled,
The four field sward mottled,
The old white-faced,
The grey Geigen,
With the White Bull
From the court of the King;
And the little black calf
Tho' suspended on the hook,
Come though also, quite well home.

The words of the Lady of the Lake in the Legend of Llyn-y-fan Fach, recorded in *The Physicians of Myddfai* published in 1843. She calls her cattle back to the depths of the lake from where they, and she, had come. She surely refers to the White Park bull at nearby Dinefwr and, perhaps, the black calf the breed sometimes produces as a throwback to their ancient roots in the original wild auroch.

Grazing the slopes beneath Dinefwr Castle

Welsh Harlequin Ducks

Welsh Harlequin drake.

The common wild mallard duck is the ancestor of all modern breeds and by the tenth century in Wales they had been domesticated enough to feature in Welsh law. In fact, experts believe that the duck was probably domesticated before the chicken, although no one can say for sure.

We have no idea what tenth-century Welsh ducks looked like, but it's a fair guess to say they probably looked something like a mallard. The medieval monasteries are thought to have taken selective duck breeding to a new level, with specific meat and egg-laying breeds being developed. By 1885, William Cook, author of *Poultry Breeder and Feeder*, asserted: 'In a few years duck-keeping will become a general thing.'

He was wrong about that, but by World War I the Indian Runner breed, originating in the East Indies, was capable of producing 200 eggs a year. And the Runners were one of the ancestors of one of only two distinct Welsh breeds – the Welsh Harlequin.

This was developed in 1949 from two sorts of Khaki Campbell stock – a type first developed in Gloucestershire by crossing an Indian Runner and a Rouen drake – and is Welsh by adoption rather than strict geographical origin.

The man behind the breed was Group Captain Leslie Bonnet, who originally embarked on his project in Hertfordshire in 1949, but continued the breeding programme under the name Welsh Harlequin after the family moved to Cricieth in north Wales.

His flock was decimated one night in 1968 by a fox when the family neglected to shut them away securely and all Leslie Bonnet's work was nearly lost.

But a Lancashire man called Eddie Grayson saved the day. He had bought some of the Group Captain's original Welsh Harlequins in 1963, and when he heard about the disaster he wrote up and promoted a standard for the breed and formed a club. The standard was accepted in 1987.

> '**The worth of a duck is one legal penny.**
> **The worth of a hen or a cock is one cut penny.**'

The quote, from the ancient Laws of Wales passed down to us from the tenth-century southern Welsh King Hywel Dda (Hywel the Good) in a thirteenth-century text, shows that ducks were domesticated by that time and considered more valuable than a chicken. A 'cut' penny was one that had been divided to make a halfpence. The silver penny was the only coin at the time, and the Law of Hywel Dda ruled that a cut halfpenny was reckoned at three to the penny, not two.

The Welsh Harlequin is the most brightly plumaged of the lighter breeds, is of a medium size and reputed to be happy, docile and inquisitive. Drakes typically reach 5-5.5lbs (2.25-2.5 kg) and ducks 4.5-5lbs (2-2.25 kg). The drake has a green and bronze head, a white ring around the neck, speckled white and mahogany red on the breast and shoulders, a tortoiseshell effect on the wings and a creamy white underbody. They have orange legs. The duck has a honey-brown head and neck and a body that changes from fawn to cream, with a light brown rump, with the same tortoiseshell effect on her wings.

They are docile and placid, good layers and reasonable mothers. They make sociable back-garden ducks because they don't fly well but forage earnestly. They are dual purpose, usually laying between 100 and 150 eggs a year – though some strains can produce 200 – and they produce a reasonable carcass for the table. There were thought to be only 80 breeding females in Britain in 2002.

Colin and Jaquie Rouse.

Dr Colin Rouse, a retired college lecturer, has bred Welsh Harlequin ducks for decades and says they delight the visitors who take bed-and-breakfast in the Georgian farmhouse where he lives with his wife Jacquie near Carmarthen. The ducks run free-range on two acres of gardens and orchards together with chickens and a pair of Brecon Buff geese.

'I started keeping them because I thought they were very pretty,' he says.

His original stock came from north Wales from a breeder who was giving up his hobby and who had bought his original birds direct from Group Captain Bonnet. Colin started to incubate his own stock in 1981.

'I almost lost the lot one year thanks to a dog and a fox, but I had sold some earlier to the Museum of Welsh Life at St Fagans so I got in touch with them and had some back and carried on breeding,' he says.

The problem for breeders, as any of them will tell you, is to overcome consanguinity or inbreeding, which can lead to genetic defects and ill-health. Colin makes sure he overcomes this by occasionally buying in new unrelated stock.

'I bought two pairs a few years ago from a chap in north Wales who had won quite a few awards with his ducks so that was fresh blood. I didn't incubate any eggs in 2008 but I will be doing so this year to make sure I have enough stock and to make sure they don't get too inbred.'

Colin and Jacquie now have 15 Welsh Harlequins, which they say are easy to keep and 'much more interesting' than the geese or the chickens.

'They all have individual characters and at this time of year in the winter they all run together, but once they start breeding they separate off into three groups,' says Colin.

Two very old ducks and a drake stick together, four ducks and four drakes reared from eggs in 2007 make another group, and the 2006 newcomers from north Wales go off on their own. And living up to their reputation for a high libido, they all get aggressive once the breeding season begins, offering an action-packed, incident-filled scenario for onlookers.

And they lay well. 'Once they start to lay in early spring they carry on through to late summer and early autumn and when the drakes are 16 weeks old they kill out oven-ready at about 4lbs, so they are a useful bird,' says Colin.

And even more Welsh . . .

The Magpie duck was standardised in 1926 after being developed by the Rev M. C. Gower Williams and the delightfully named Oliver Drake in the early years of the twentieth century, probably from black and white birds in west Wales.

The handsome dual-purpose breed can lay 180 quite large eggs a year and makes a good table bird. The plumage should be white with two darker coloured areas from the shoulders to the tail and on the top of the head. There are both black-and-white and blue-and-white varieties.

Chewy, pictured right, is kept as a much-loved pet, its owners keeping a lively pictorial blog of its exploits on flickr.com.

BRECON BUFF GEESE

Mike and Chris Ashton came across the Brecon Buff goose by chance. Their daughter Rachel, known as Tig, was given a pair of female goslings, two weeks old, for her tenth birthday at Easter, 1981. They were intended to be reared for the Christmas table but they were very tame and the family fell in love with them.

'We put them in a little coop and they were so nice they became pets. They used to sit in Tig's lap and she would cradle them under her coat. We had them until they were 14 and 16,' recalls Chris.

They were followed by a trio of similar commercial white goslings. Eggs were hatched but no one wanted to buy the goslings for a reasonable price – except for eating.

'We decided that was not where we wanted to go,' says Mike. 'Chris decided she wanted a rare breed and the Brecon Buff was the obvious one. It's Welsh, it's not too big or too small, converts pasture well into meat and it's very hardy.'

But during the 1980s it was difficult to find Brecons. The Ashtons, who were both teachers at the time, searched the length and breadth of Britain for geese with the characteristic – and unique –

pink feet and bill of the Brecon Buff. Mike recalls pulling out of an auction when the price reached £140 for three birds at a rare-breeds sale in 1984.

'They were very hard to find but in the end we found some in Wales and some in Lancashire,' says Chris. 'We ended up breeding a lot in the 1980s because there were so few around. We must have populated a lot of Britain with Brecon Buffs, but we don't know how many people are still breeding them now because a lot of people who keep birds don't belong to any organisation that records what they do.'

Fortunately the breed became popular and much sought after as a pet. Hand-reared Brecons can be very tame, and the goose is an excellent sitter and mother. Brecon Buffs are now, thanks to a lot of hard work by Chris, recognised by DEFRA as a rare breed, which means there are only a few hundred breeding females.

The Ashtons, who specialise in rare-breed waterfowl within a three-acre fox-proof fence on their nine-acre smallholding near Welshpool, have half-a-dozen females and two males and say they could sell the breeding pairs they rear three times over at £100 a pair in a market where an ordinary goose for the Christmas table fetches £30.

'We don't want to over-charge but we know that if someone pays £100 for something they will look after it, but if it costs £10 they might just chuck it out,' says Mike. 'The more you charge, the better people will look after it.'

The Ashtons are among the top waterfowl breeders and judges in the UK. They gained British Waterfowl Association Exhibitor of the Year awards in 1987, and from 1996 to 1999. Chris and Mike are both BWA judges in all sections of waterfowl and have written seven books, including Chris's standard seminal *Domestic Geese*.

Chris represented the British Waterfowl Association on a DEFRA committee working on the 2006 animal-welfare legislation, and is currently helping to draw up specific guidelines for looking after birds. They gave up their teaching jobs at Welshpool to concentrate on a hobby that had grown into a second career. 'We decided that our teaching careers were a second string to living in a place in Wales where we wanted to live with waterfowl,' says Mike.

Their books have earned them world renown and the couple spent three all-expenses-paid weeks in Australia in 2008 as specialist judges at the Canberra Show and giving talks to waterfowl enthusiasts.

With up to 180 mostly rare breeds of geese and ducks on their smallholding and a high profile in the wider world of waterfowl, the Ashtons are cautious about publicising their location because they are aware that a fox-proof fence is no barrier to a determined rare waterfowl thief. 'We know people who have had expensive rare birds stolen. Although they don't have a huge market value they have a high value to their owners, and if you lose good stock it's hard to replace,' they say.

They regard their Brecon Buffs as special. 'The first ones we had had a fantastic temperament. They were bomb-proof. And if you have them as goslings they will follow you around and talk to you. They will come into the kitchen. They are wonderful,' said Chris.

The Brecon Buff is one of the few breeds of geese originating in the UK and was the first to be standardised. Rhys Llewellyn from Swansea was responsible. He noticed buff-coloured geese on hill farms in the Brecon Beacons and used this stock to develop his buff geese, which were recognised by the Poultry Club as a breed in 1934.

Llewellyn purposely kept his geese in testing conditions, ranging freely on a wide area of grass. The aim was to produce a hardy, medium-weight goose which was able to look after itself on the farm – as long as it was protected from foxes.

The result is a compact, medium-size, plump and round-breasted table bird. Buff birds are still popular on farms and smallholdings in Wales today because they grow well on free-range grazing and are less aggressive than the commercial white goose. They are also easier to dress for the table than white or grey geese.

Exhibition Brecons are beautiful birds with a deep and even shade of buff body feathers, edged with a lighter shade, and dark brown eyes. They are the only British breed with pink feet and beaks, a characteristic of domestic geese which have evolved from the Eastern Greylag. All other British breeds have orange legs and beak, which is a characteristic of the Western Greylag. Experts believe it unlikely that Welsh hill farmers would have imported Pomeranian breeding stock, but some wild geese that over-winter in Wales have pinkish feet and buff-tinged feathering.

Weights range from 16-20lbs in the gander and 14-18lbs in the goose. They are good mothers and rarely fly. The bird is active and alert and exceptionally hardy, but docile in temperament and with a tendency to become very tame.

In 2002 there were thought to be 50 breeding females.

'But they are not all like that. We have to buy in some new blood from time to time to avoid inbreeding and we had one strain that were absolute pigs, but since then we've been able to get good-tempered stock.'

Chris says commercial white geese are trouble and give the wider world of geese a bad name. 'We don't recommend people to get them because they've not been bred to be amenable, but a lot of people still buy them as a hobby.'

'There's quite a demand for Brecon Buffs from breeders and as pet birds but these are not Bernard Matthews turkeys. We don't eat them, any more than dog owners would eat their family pet, and we have never sold for the table. We have killed the odd bird in the past, but we didn't like doing it.'

Traditions and Folklore

The goose has a legendary reputation for being a silly bird, hence the phrase 'a silly goose'. And if a goose flies around the house it is said to be a death omen. If it hisses or quacks more than normal, rain is on the way.

But the goose is also associated with wealth. The English proverb warns: 'Kill not the goose that lays the golden eggs.' And an old rhyme claims:

'Whosoever eats goose on Michaelmas Day, Shall never lack money his debts to pay.'

One country tradition claims that the presence of geese on the farm is proof that the wife wears the trousers. Keeping poultry was always woman's work, and the proverb suggests that no man would allow such a filthy bird to foul his pastures – although goose dung is actually less mucky than that of sheep or cattle.

In the Middle Ages the goose was an important part of the farm economy, providing crucial commodities like goose fat, quills for writing and feathers for arrows. A goose wing was a handy household implement for cleaning out under the dresser.

There were once thousands of geese in Wales, and they were gathered by farmers and drovers in country towns where they were driven through a mix of tar and sand to protect their feet as they were walked long distances, at a pace of around two miles an hour to markets in the cities. A proverb from Mid Glamorganshire collected in 1906 refers to a similar practice – '*Dysgu dy fam-gu i bedoli whid*' (teaching your grandmother to shoe ducks).

The goose was the traditional Christmas meal until turkey began to appear in Britain in the late nineteenth century.

WELSH COBS

Roscoe and Elin Lloyd packing the Prince of Wales Cup for its return to the Royal Welsh.

One of the greatest sights in rural Wales is the running of the Welsh cobs at the Royal Welsh Show every July. Handlers race around the main show ring at full pelt, leading the powerful and graceful stallions and mares of a breed described as the most versatile and beautiful in the world.

'The Welsh cob is not a true horse or pony; it is unique in being a Welsh cob, combining the very best qualities of both,' says Ifor Lloyd of the famous Derwen Stud. Ifor has raced cobs around the main ring on numerous occasions and horses from his stud have lifted the top Royal Welsh Show cob prize, the George Prince of Wales Cup, no fewer than 13 times – more than anyone else.

'Some say the cob was brought here by the Romans and others that it evolved from the mountain pony. But I've got a feeling – even though there's no historical basis for it –that the cob has been on the Welsh hills for thousands of years.'

Ifor Lloyd runs the famous stud on a 230-acre farm at Ynyshir, Pennant near Aberaeron with his wife Myfanwy and their son Dyfed. He grew up among cobs in a farming family that was steeped in the tradition. His grandfather and great-uncle were among the founders of the Welsh Pony and Cob Society in 1901 and the Derwen Stud dates back to 1944 when Ifor's father Roscoe bought a ten-year-old 14.1hh black mare called Dewi Rosina at Llanybydder's famous horse sale.

The mare, bred by JO Davies of Pentre-brain, Tregaron, won seven prizes, including championships at Cardigan, Llangwyryfon and Crugybar in 1946, five first-prizes in 1947 including the championships at Lampeter and Llangwyryfon and a second prize at the Royal Welsh Show. She was second again at the Royal Welsh Show in 1949 and finally won the top prize there in 1951 at the age of 17. Her last appearance at the Royal Welsh came in 1953 when Roscoe Lloyd ran her around the showground to the supreme championship and her name was engraved on the George, Prince of Wales Cup – the first of the stud's all-time record of 13 wins of the breed's top prize.

Dewi Rosina produced top-quality foals and became the foundation of the Derwen Stud, which was named after the family farm, Derwen Fawr, at Crugybar in north Carmarthenshire. Her descendants can now be found all over the globe.

The Welsh cob has evolved over many centuries and is renowned for its courage, tractability and powers of endurance. Praised in medieval literature, the cob is extremely versatile and an ideal multi-purpose farm animal. It could do all the farm work and take the farmer and his family to church and market. Welsh cobs carried shepherds over the Welsh mountains for centuries, and some still do.

Captain TA Howson, secretary of the WPCS from 1928 to 1948, described the cob as follows:

'As the very name implies, a Welsh cob must be a short-legged animal of Herculean strength. In build it is distinctly the dual-purpose ride and drive type, combining quality activity, and a spirited yet kindly temperament with a subtle "personality" entirely its own. It may be anything from under 14 to something over 15 hands in height and shows much pony character all over, but especially about the head and forehand and in the silky forelock, mane and heel tufts. Viewed from the front a cob should display some width of chest and from behind the thighs must be extremely powerful and full – a split-up silty looking cob is an abomination. It must walk quickly and collectedly and its trotting paces must be very forceful, free and fast, with every joint in use. It must get away in front with full play on the shoulders, knees well up, with forelegs straightened out and feet brought lightly to the ground, without the slightest tendency to drop upon the heels. The hocks must be flexed vigorously and the hind legs switched electrically beneath the body in order to support the weight, give proper balance, and provide propulsive power. The action should be straight and true all round, although a few exceptionally fast trotters are inclined to go a trifle wide behind.'

Ifor Lloyd with Derwen Groten Goch.

Nebo Black Magic at work in London, but Derwen owners brought him back to Wales, where he became a champion Welsh cob himself and sired outstanding offspring.

The stud relocated from Crugybar to Pennant in 1963 because the family doctor said sea air would benefit the health of Ifor's mother, Elin. Ifor and Myfanwy took over management of the stud in 1974, developing bloodlines that have proved popular all over the world. Over the past few decades, Derwen cobs have been sold to eighteen countries, including Sweden, Pakistan and Canada.

When Ifor and Myfanwy held a reduction sale in September, 2008, a crowd of 2,000 turned up and 46 cobs were sold at an average of £2,600 for the mares, £1,547 for young females, £1,160 for foals and £831 for geldings. One 20-year-old mare fetched more than £3,000. Eleven of the horses went to Scandinavia and others to France and Finland as well as to all parts of Britain.

'We're getting on and we had to cut back to make it a bit easier, so we have some empty stables now and we're able to relax a bit more,' says Ifor. 'But all you really have in life is health and we hope to be able to carry on for years.'

The stud has not put horses in the show ring for seven years, since Ifor became chairman of the Welsh Pony and Cob Society. He was a member of the society's ruling council before stepping down in 2005, but has not returned to the ring. Instead he is in great demand as a local, national and international judge at agricultural and horse shows – and as an after-dinner speaker. Ifor and Myfanwy's story of the Derwen Stud cobs, *Winning Welsh Cobs*, was published by Gomer in 2008.

'The cob is a wonderful breed – in fact all four sections of the Welsh breed are wonderful animals,' says Ifor. 'The cob is so versatile and it has a wonderful temperament. It's not going to compete with the thoroughbred in the Derby, but it's for your general Joe Bloggs who has not necessarily got top skills, and it will do for all members of the family, whatever the age. Families can't afford to buy more than one horse these days and they can all ride the Welsh cob.'

Ifor is evangelical about the breed and believes more should be done to promote it across the world. There is already a strong following in Sweden, mostly thanks to Derwen Stud exports, with 300 members of the Welsh Pony and Cob Society there. It sounds a lot until you realise that the Shetland Pony Club has 1,800 Swedish members. 'People in Wales think everyone knows about the Welsh cob, but they don't,' says Ifor.

The stud now has a museum at Pennant where a large collection of agricultural and equine artefacts can be seen by visitors. The centre also catalogues the history of the stud and its horses and serves as a venue for charity concerts and Welsh-language television's popular variety programme, *Noson Lawen*.

The first written references to ponies and cobs in Wales appeared in the laws of Hywel Dda (Hywel the Good), ruler of Deheubarth. The Laws, written in the year 930, mention three types of horses and ponies in Wales: the Palfrey or riding pony; the Rowney or Sumpter, which was the pack horse; and the working horse that pulled the sledge or small gambo – the cob.

The Welsh cob is an ancient breed descended from the tough native mountain ponies of Wales. Evidence of the existence of the Welsh cob in the middle ages and even earlier can be found in past ages' literature and pictures. Poetry of fifteenth-century Welsh poets describes horses in Wales at that period and those descriptions would fit the ideal type of Welsh cob in Wales five hundred years later.

The poet Guto'r Glyn also refers to pedigrees of stallions, tracing them back to romances and the steeds of Arthur of the round table. Wales is the only nation in Europe which can refer to horses' pedigrees between 1200 and 1600.

'Mab i'r Du, ymhob erw deg, O Bryndyn o bai redeg . . .'

He is the son of 'Du o Bryndyn'
He would win the race in any fair field;
His mother was daughter to the stallion of
Anglesey which carried eight people.
They are descendants to Du'r Moroedd
And I know that he is one of them.
He is nephew to Myngwyn Ial.
In Powys no fetter could hold him.
He is of the stock of Ffwg Warin's stallion,
And that stock grinds its fodder small
With its strong jaws.
He is a stallion of the highest pedigree
In Anglesey,
From the line of Talebolion.

'Pedigree of a Welsh Cob', translated from the Welsh of Guto'r Glyn (c.1445-75)

Tudor Aled, a famous Welsh poet of the early sixteenth century, wrote several poems describing a Welsh cob stallion called The Abbot of Aberconwy: *'Llygaid fel dwy ellygen, Llymion byw'n llamu'n 'i ben . . .'* (He has the outlook and gait of a stag, Eyes like two ripe pears, Bulging and dancing in his head, A dished face, a wide forehead, his coat like new silk . . .)

He was a river-leaper,
A roebuck's leap from a snake;
He'd faced whatever he wished:
If rafter try to clear it;
There's no need, to make him leap,
For steel against his belly.
With a keen horseman, no clod,
He would know his intention.
If he's sent over a fence,
He will run, the lord's stallion,
Bold jumper where thorns grow thick,
Full of spikes, in Llaneurgain.
Best ever, when set running,
Fine steed to steal a fair girl.
Here awaits me a maiden,
Fair girl, if I have a horse.

'Welsh Cob Stallion', translated from the Welsh of Tudor Aled (1480-1526)

WELSH PONIES

Welsh cob mare Sian Gwalia, owned by Mr L.O. Williams, shown by Mr E.S. Davies. Reserve for the George Prince of Wales Cup, Royal Welsh Shows 1934 and 1936.

Ponies probably roamed the hills of Wales in prehistoric times. The sparse vegetation and shelter of their natural habitat in the hills and mountains produced a tough, hardy pony and today's Welsh Mountain Pony is thought to be descended from the original Celtic pony crossed with animals brought to Britain by the Romans.

But the pony's survival into modern times is remarkable and a testament to its sharp intelligence and hardiness. Ponies soon multiplied so successfully that they became an agricultural pest as they ran wild across the hills, being considered such a nuisance that farmers hunted them down. More trouble arrived in the sixteenth century when King Henry VIII ruled that only horses capable of being used in battle were of any use and ordered the destruction of all stallions under 15 hands and all mares under 13 hands. On the face of it, the little Welsh Mountain Pony, standardised in modern times at 12 hands and two inches, had no chance. But many escaped into the hills and inaccessible forests of the uplands.

The harsh climate and continual persecution helped to create a very hardy animal with plenty of bone, and a thick mane, coat and tail. The ponies were predominantly dark, with blacks, browns and dark duns being the hardiest.

Once they were caught and tamed, the ponies were used for a variety of duties. They were commonly employed as pit ponies in the mines and for general use as pack animals, and their temperament made them popular driving ponies.

They have had a strong influence on other types of pony, including the early Thoroughbred, Hackney, Hunter and British Riding pony. King Edward VII is said to have encouraged the use of Welsh ponies as polo mounts.

E.S. Davies (Wynne's father) driving Dinarth What Ho at Llandeilo Show 1951.

Today Welsh ponies are considered ideal for children and are so popular worldwide that there are breed societies in twelve overseas countries.

One of its greatest champions is Wynne the Voice, Royal Welsh Show commentator. Dr Wynne Davies of the Ceulan Stud from Miskin, Pontyclun, is a world authority on Welsh horses; his family has been closely involved in the development of all four sections of the Welsh Stud Book, from Welsh Mountain Pony to Welsh cob.

Author of many books, this Doctor of Philosophy and former head of chemistry at the Cardiff Institute is an honorary Life President of the Welsh Pony and Cob Society, whose patron is the Queen. He received the MBE for services to the breed.

Dr Davies can trace the bloodline of his Ceulan Stud of Welsh Mountain Ponies back to Klondyke, a mare bred by his great-great-uncle John Thomas in 1894. His grandparents, L. O. Williams and Annie Williams, exhibited at the first Royal Welsh Show in 1904. His granddaughter Leah is now the sixth generation of the family to handle the breed.

'My grandparents actually competed against each other in 1904. I don't know why, because they were married at the time, but it must have been a friendly contest,' says Wynne.

Wynne's father, Evan Samuel Davies, from Talybont near Aberystwyth, first competed at the Royal Welsh Show in 1926, and won a section championship in 1928 with Seren Ceulan. This mare produced foals that were exported to Australia and the Argentine – as well as pulling a cart delivering feed to farms around the Cardiganshire villages of Talybont, Borth and Eglwysfach.

Wynne competed – and won – in the Royal Welsh for the first time in 1947 at the age of 14, helping his father to show the Section A stallion Dinarth What Ho. And two years later the family won three of the main prizes, with outstanding examples in all four of the main Welsh Pony and Cob breed sections.

Dr Wynne Davies with W. A. Simpson, editor of the US magazine *Your Pony*, in 1956, on a gate at Blaendyrin, Sennybridge.

Sunwillow Irving, driven by Emma Edwards at the 2008 Royal Welsh Show, where they won 2nd prize.

'From the 1970s onwards, we won the Section A progeny competition for groups of three ponies no less than 11 times – setting a record. I think they eventually stopped the competition because it was becoming a bit predictable,' says Wynne. 'We have bred from different stallions but have kept the female lines, which are nearly all related, and which go back to Klondyke in 1894.'

Away from the stud, Wynne is a prolific writer. He has reported for *Horse and Hound* since 1954 and has been a commentator in the main ring at the Royal Welsh since 1976, although he came out of show-ring retirement in 2000 to show his all-time favourite pony, Ceulan Cariad.

'My son David has taken over the competing side of things now while I concentrate on the ringside commentary. It's an early start at 7.30 in the morning and we don't finish until 7 o'clock at night,' he says.

'My wife says although she doesn't see me for the duration of the show, she's got to listen to me all day. If there's a sudden silence, she gets a bit concerned that I've keeled over.'

The size and shape of fragments of a harness and chariot wheels in an Iron Age hoard discovered in Llyn Cerrig Bach on Anglesey, when workmen were constructing the Valley airfield during World War Two, show that the Celts used ponies rather than horses between the shafts of the chariots that so impressed Julius Caesar with their speed and manoeuvrability.

Caesar is thought to have founded a stud on the shores of Lake Bala and was so impressed with the native pony that he took some back to Rome with him. The Romans brought ponies of their own when they occupied Britain, presumably Arabians, which bred with the native ponies to produce hardy but very beautiful offspring.

When the Romans left Britain in the fifth century, many of their own ponies were turned loose or sold to locals, allowing another strong injection of Arab blood.

More Arabian influences arrived in the Middle Ages with ponies brought home by Welsh crusader knights and these traits are clearly present in the modern Welsh Mountain Pony with its beautiful dished face and delicate muzzle.

Top: Wynne's grandchildren (*left to right*): Rachel, Joseph, Leah and Miriam with their father David, and Ceulan Ceryl.

Centre: Dr Wynne showing his prize-winning, Section A stallion, Trefaes Taran, at Lampeter Welsh Breeds Show.

Below: Wynne Davies showing Dinarth What Ho at the 1952 Royal Welsh Show.

In 1901, landowners and farmers in Wales recognised the importance of keeping pedigree records and founded the Welsh Pony and Cob Society. One year later, the first stud book was published.

Today the Queen herself is patron of a society that has thousands of members across the world, and the stud book is currently in its 80th volume.

Welsh Mountain Ponies are ridden and driven all over the world and are equally at home in the cold climates of places like Sweden and Canada, or in the heat of Africa and Australia. But the semi-feral Welsh Mountain Pony, the basis of the stud book, and the world's most beautiful pony, is under threat in its homeland amid the hills of Wales.

New European Commission regulations aiming to ensure traceability in the European horse-meat market, creates a financial and administrative headache that herd owners say is not worth the time and money. Each pony must have an individual passport and a microchip inserted by a vet.

There is a strong lobby in Wales which urges the Welsh Assembly Government to seek derogation from the ruling, on the lines of one already agreed for the New Forest ponies of England.

SHEEP: LLANWENOG

Elfyn Morgan was just eight years old when he was given his first ewe. It was an old broken-mouthed Llanwenog, given to him by 'Uncle Enoch' from the farm next door where Elfyn used to help out in his spare time. In the first year she produced two ewe lambs and the following year a couple of rams. Elfyn's close association with the local breed of sheep had begun.

'Dad took on another piece of land and took on the sheep and we kept the best. I grew up with them,' he says. The old ewe produced one ram that sold for £150 and lived on until she was seven or eight, and the best of the matriarch's flock, sired by the neighbour's ram for the first two or three years, turned out to be good enough for Elfyn to win three breed championships.

Many years later Elfyn still keeps a flock of 30 Llanwenog sheep on his 248-acre rented farm, Glwydwern, in Llanwnen, on the Carmarthenshire/ Cardiganshire border, just a few miles from the village that gave the breed its name.

'We keep a few for sentimental reasons as much as anything and we run them with the other flock of 480 Beulahs, although they prefer to be on their own. They are a quiet ewe compared with the Beulah Speckled Face.'

The Beulah, or Epynt Hill Breed as it used to be known on the Breckonshire uplands where it originated, is another of the dozen or so Welsh breeds of sheep still reared commercially by Welsh farmers.

The Llanwenog has become known as a smallholder's ewe and intense interest from across the border has lifted the animal off the rare-breed register

'Smallholders from England come down with big money and take good stock back, and we never see the offspring,' says Elfyn. 'They are good quality ewes and produce lambs as good as any. A lot of people use them to cross with the Texel but I keep them pure, with one or two rams to improve the flock.'

Elfyn and his wife Sharon are well known in the farming world, having won the prestigious Group of Three supreme championship with their Beulah Speckled Face at the Royal Welsh Show. Sharon's grandfather, David Jones of Blaenblodau, New Inn, Pencader, is a renowned breeder of Beulahs, and the winner of numerous championships, including the Royal Welsh. His great-grandchildren, Daniel aged 11, Gethin, 8 and Nia, 5 are the coming generation in a rich family tradition of rearing sheep.

The Llanwenog sheep are typical of the breeds developed by farmers in a particular place and at a particular time, who found that the breed worked extremely well in the localised conditions. The Llanwenog venture began when some of the landowning gentry in the Teifi Valley took advantage of the arrival of the railway in the 1870s to import Shropshire Down sheep.

These lowland sheep were very different from the local hill ewe, a now extinct horned blackface known as the Llanllwni after the moorland mountain where it was largely kept. The landlords encouraged their tenants to use the Shropshire Down rams on their sheep and the result was a polled, blackface ewe that combined the qualities of both – the wool, meat and conformation of the Shropshire Down accompanied by the hardiness and milkiness of the Llanllwni.

And so it remained, a local curiosity virtually unknown outside the Teifi Valley until 1957 when local farmers established the Llanwenog Sheep Society to promote and develop the breed. The move paid off within a few years when the wider sheep world was suddenly forced to pay attention.

First there was a succession of wins in national lambing competitions in the 1960s, with a lambing percentage of a staggering 215% on no fewer than six occasions. And farmers really sat up and took notice when the results were published of flock recording by the Meat and Livestock Commission in the 1970s. These showed that the Llanwenog was the most prolific native breed – and the only British breed to top a 200% lambing rate. These days an average of 180% lambs reared to ewes tupped can be expected under commercial conditions. This success rate led English farmers to involve the Llanwenog in the creation of the Cambridge breed.

Daniel, Gethin and Nia Morgan.

The Llanwenog is designated as 'semi-lowland'. That means it will thrive on land up to 1,000ft above sea level, but is big enough to take advantage of better lowland pasture. The ewes are very hardy and will thrive at more than 1,000ft above sea level but because they are not a true hill breed, the lambs are not born with the type of coat which helps them to survive at a greater height. These days, when farmers tend to opt for indoor lambing, that is no longer so important. But it can affect how quickly the lambs can be turned out if the land is very high and exposed.

The Llanwenog is also renowned for its placid temperament. It is no wonder that children enjoy handling this animal. It does not have the wanderlust of some breeds and is easily handled and readily contained.

Many of the larger breeders put the best of their Llanwenog ewes to a pure-bred Llanwenog ram in order to obtain their ewe replacements, and the remainder to terminal sire to produce cross-breed meat lambs. Terminal sire breeds used on the Llanwenog will produce a fast-finishing good-quality lamb at a popular dead weight, of around 16-18kg.

Interest in the breed increased dramatically after it was listed by the Rare Breeds Survival Trust in 1994 and the number of registered flocks now approaches the all-time high of the 1960s. RBST assistance for a range of breed-improvement projects and the creation of the English Support Group helped to establish many new flocks across England and Wales. In 2006 there were nearly 4,000 Llanwenog ewes, 55% up on 1994, and another 1,336 ewe lambs were retained. The 99 registered flocks compared with just 42 in 1994.

There is now a second sale of stock at Melton Mowbray and new marketing initiatives in rare-breed meat and wool offer further opportunities for the breed. The wool is rated as one of the finest in the UK. Fleeces average 2.5kg and are especially sought after by hand-spinners.

Sheep: Welsh Mountain

Welsh Mountain ram.

Tan-faced sheep have inhabited the hills and mountains of Wales for two thousand years – since the Romans imported white-faced animals and crossed them with the Soay-type animal they found when they arrived in Britain. This is probably the most important Welsh breed and a parent to numerous other types. Today the term is a general one for many of the indigenous Welsh breeds and there are many distinct varieties. The main ones are the original Hardy Welsh Mountain, the Black Welsh Mountain, the South Wales Mountain, and the Badger Face Welsh Mountain with its sub-divisions of Torddu (black belly) and Torwen (white belly), and the Balwen.

The Hardy Welsh Mountain ewe has a white or tan face. Its strong, close-textured fleece can weigh up to 2kg. The ram is usually, but not always, horned. An average mature ewe weighs 35-40kg on the mountain but can add a further 10kg when accommodated on lowland pasture. It is well adapted to the harsh environment of the uplands, where the short, thick wool helps resists heavy rain and bitter weather, and it is able to survive on poor pasture in conditions where other breeds could not thrive. The sheep are smaller than many, and therefore produce a smaller carcass and smaller joints of meat.

Black Welsh Mountain sheep are an ancient breed characterised by their hardiness, self-reliance and disease resistance. Hill flocks are easy to keep in normal conditions, requiring no supplementary feeding. They thrive on the short rough grasses and herbage of the unploughed uplands. An average mature ewe weighs 45kg, while the rams range from 60kg to 65kg. They are good mothers and produce premium quality, lean meat with an excellent meat-to-bone ratio and a full flavour.

The South Wales Mountain or Nelson looks similar to the other Welsh Mountain breeds but is larger than any of them. The mature rams, which are usually horned, weigh up to 85kg and the hornless ewes up to 55kg. The breed is native to the hill areas of south Powys, Carmarthenshire, Monmouthshire and Glamorgan, and has been reared on the south Wales uplands for generations. Like all the mountain sheep, it is extremely hardy and can thrive on harsh hill pastures. It is long-lived and easy to manage. The Nelson is white with tan markings on face and legs and often has a distinctive brown collar. The fleece is dense with an even mixture of white, kempy fibre making it highly weather resistant. There is little wool on the belly, which reduces susceptibility to flystrike. It matures early to produce a lean carcass of excellent flavour. The flock book was established in the early 1980s.

The Badger Face Welsh Mountain is an ancient breed of hardy sheep that can adjust to any system and produce a high percentage of twins and some triplets in favourable conditions. Torddu, the Welsh name meaning 'black belly', has distinct black stripes above the eyes and a black stripe running from under the chin to the belly and on to the end of the tail. The legs are black with a tan stripe. The fleece can be white, grey or light brown. The wool is firm and of medium length (7-10 cm). The Torwen, the Welsh name meaning 'white belly', shows the reverse colouring, but with a smaller eye stripe. It is compact and strong and of medium size. Both Torddu and Torwen rams are horned and weigh up to 90kg. Ewes are polled and weigh up to 60kg. The Badger Face is long-lived and easily managed and produces lean and tender meat. The animal is hardy and thrifty, and the ewes lamb easily and have plentiful milk, which helps to produce strong, fast-growing lambs. It is suitable both for smallholders and for lowland or hill farmers and the fleece is popular with hand-spinners and others

who like the naturally coloured wool, but it is used mostly for carpets.

The Balwen Welsh Mountain is a sheep for all seasons. One of the original Welsh breeds of sheep, the Balwen is one of the most striking and versatile of all the rare breeds. The sheep has a base colour of black, dark brown or dark grey, with a white stripe running from the poll of the head to the top of the nose – Balwen means 'white blaze'. The feet and the lower half or two-thirds of the tail are white. Rams are horned and ewes polled. The average mature ewe weighs 40-50kgs and the rams are 45-60kgs. They were once found only in the extremely remote area of the Upper Tywi valley, an area of about 50 square miles on the borders of Carmarthenshire and Breconshire. They were nearly wiped out in the disastrous winter of 1947, when only one ram survived, but during the 1950s and 1960s there was a steady revival and in the 1970s people outside the valley began to take an interest in the breed. The Balwen Welsh Mountain Breed Society was formed in 1985, and the breed has now expanded far beyond its native valley.

Balwen sheep at Nangaredig in the Tywi valley.

SHEEP: WELSH MULE
AND OTHER CROSS-BREEDS

> " *To live in Wales*
> *is to love sheep*
> *and be afraid*
> *of dragons* "
>
> Peter Finch, 'A Welsh Wordscape'

Sheep are thought to have been the first animals to be domesticated by human beings, some 9,000 years ago, and were probably brought to Britain by Neolithic settlers during the Third Millennium BC.

The animal they brought was likely to have been the brown Soay sheep, which is still found in some areas. The Romans brought a white sheep with finer wool, and this is the animal many believe to be the ancestor of our many modern breeds. Crossed with the Soay, it was the ancestor of today's Welsh Mountain sheep, although the Romans concentrated on developing an animal that produced fine wool. Mutton, let alone lamb, was seldom on the menu.

Black-faced breeds came with the Vikings in the eighth and ninth centuries, and further development came from the monks who built religious houses across the country. The Cistercians in particular bred sheep and made great strides in developing agricultural systems. Again, it was the production of wool for clothing – and milk for the human consumption – that represented the economic value of the sheep in the medieval monastic world. (In today's financial climate, farmers struggle to make enough from their fleeces to pay the cost of shearing.) Wool and woollen products were the mainstay of the British economy from the twelfth to the eighteenth century – until industrialisation changed the country forever. Its historic importance is the reason why the Lord Chancellor in the House of Lords sits on the Woolsack.

The Middle Ages also saw sheep brought to moveable folds at night to improve the land by treading in their manure.

In Wales, the hardy Welsh Mountain is the common ancestor of all the country's distinctive breeds, and it is still the most numerous and economically important, converting the sparse pasture of the uplands into meat that is prized for its taste. The earliest detailed descriptions date from the late eighteenth century and since then the breed has evolved into three distinct types – the hardy Welsh Mountain, which is mostly confined to north Wales, the larger Pedigree Aberystwyth or Improved Welsh Mountain and, largest of all, the South Wales Mountain, formerly known as the Nelson.

Other Welsh upland breeds are the Black Mountain, the Badger-faced or Torddu (literally black-bellied), the Beulah Speckled Face, the

Brecknock Hill Cheviot (brought from Scotland in the nineteenth century), and the Hill Radnor.

As well as these there are the established crossed breeds. The Welsh Halfbred is produced by putting a Border Leicester ram to a Welsh Mountain ewe and the Welsh Mule is the result of a Bluefaced Leicester put to a hill ewe. Crossing also produced the grassland breeds – the Kerry Hill, the Clun Forest, the Lleyn and the Llanwenog.

The Welsh Halfbred revolutionised prospects for Welsh hill farmers when it was pioneered by a small team of progressive farmers in 1955. Welsh ewes had been crossed with Border Leicester rams since the early 1900s but it was not until the mid-1950s that the cross was given the name Welsh Halfbred and the co-operative Welsh Halfbred Sheep Breeders' Association was formed to market the ewes and ewe lambs.

The association set high standards and established centres at Ruthin, Builth Wells and Welshpool, where buyers knew they could see several thousand ewes and lambs of a uniform type and quality. Association inspectors weeded out any that did not meet the standards. The Welsh Halfbred sales were an innovation in the 1950s but were soon copied by other breed associations and are now common at all commercial ewe sales.

'We claim that the Welsh Halfbred is the ideal animal for commercial fat lamb production,' says Gordon Wilyman, the Birmingham-born Denbighshire farmer who was one of the pioneers in the 1950s. 'She combines the qualities of hardiness, longevity, ability to milk and the wonderful mothering instinct of the Welsh ewe with the growth and bold character of the Border Leicester. Our sheep are now in most of the counties of England and have crossed the border into Scotland.'

The Welsh Mule is one of the modern developments of sheep farmers in Wales. It is the progeny of a registered Bluefaced Leicester ram crossed with the Welsh Mountain, Beulah or Welsh Hill Speckled-face ewes – all hardy, healthy Welsh hill breeds which impart their best qualities to their offspring.

Even the ewe lambs produce prolific crops of lambs and their superior mothering instinct and excellent milking qualities ensure a very high percentage of live lambs reared – and pure-bred flocks sometimes producing more than three lambs per ewe.

The Mule was first developed in northern England using Swaledale ewes or other breeds like the Scottish Blackface, and the practice spread to Wales in the latter half of the twentieth century. The hardy Speckle Faced ewe seems to produce the most successful Mule. A Welsh Mule Society was formed in 1979 and the first sale attracted an entry of 4,000 ewes.

The Welsh Mule thrives in a wide range of management systems. It is easy to house and handle, it is hardy, forages well and gives farmers a relatively trouble-free lambing season. It also produces fine, high-quality wool, a legacy inherited from the Blue faced Leicester ram.

WELSH PIGS

" Cats look down on you, dogs look up to you. Only a pig treats you as equal!"

Mrs Organ Morgan,
Under Milk Wood

Up until the 1960s the Welsh Pig was one of the three most popular commercial breeds in Britain. It is now one of the rarest.

This is not because it is a difficult beast to rear or because it is a poor converter of feed into pork and bacon. On the contrary, it is hardy, easy to manage both indoors and out, fast-growing and produces exceedingly tasty meat. The decline was actually the result of a fashion for leaner meat and the growth of commercial hybrids in Britain's shrinking pig industry.

The pig was once crucial for the self-reliant Welsh farmer and cottager, many of whom seldom ate meat unless they – or a neighbour – had killed a pig. The animal was their savings bank, one of the few ways to convert kitchen waste and spare-time labour into cash, and in some parts of Wales a man's credit rating with shopkeepers depended on whether or not he kept a pig.

The custom of keeping a pig on the farm lasted into the late twentieth century, but the arrival of regulations that effectively banned on-farm killing, coupled with the decline of local abattoirs, has virtually wiped it out.

There are now only around twenty breeders, keeping a total of about 250 sows and 88 boars.

The distinctive Welsh pig, a white animal, has lop ears that almost touch the nose, and a long level body with deep strong hams and legs set well apart. George Eglington, acknowledged as the founder of the modern Welsh breed, described the perfect Welsh Pig as 'pear shaped' when viewed from either the side or from above.

It's a description that's accepted by Fiona Powell of Llanidloes, secretary of the Wales & Border Counties Pig Breeders' Association.

'They are a bit pear-shaped but there are varying shapes of pear – there's quite a lot of variation in the breed,' she says.

'We are short of blood lines at the moment, but they all have different characteristics. The Julia blood line, for instance, is hairy and quite a short pig.'

Bloodlines are a delicate subject among the small fraternity of Welsh Pig breeders. Seven female and three male bloodlines have been lost in the last few years. Only the Large Black Pig is now rarer than the Welsh.

Fiona and her husband Richard, whose 250-acre farm at Llidartywaun, Llanidloes, rises from 1,200 to 1,800 feet above sea level, have the largest herd of Welsh Pigs in Wales. Their Brynhafod Herd consists

The pig was domesticated in China 5,000 years ago and Chinese pigs soon made their way to Britain, where they contributed to the development of the British breeds.

It's clear that pigs were considered special – a tribute no doubt to their fertility and almost unequalled potential as meat producers, and they were positively revered in Wales.

According to the **Mabinogion**, pigs were introduced to Britain as a result of trickery against King Pwyll, who was standing in as Lord of the Underworld for 12 months. Pwyll's son Pryderi guarded the pigs of Pendaran Dyfed in Glyn Cuch in Emlyn.

The Welsh Triads spoke of the Three Powerful Swineherds of Britain, all with quasi magical powers and in the **Black Book of Carmarthen**, Merlin addresses one of his poems to a piglet.

Coll, son of Collfewy guarded Henwen, the sow of Dallwyr Dallben and the animal form of

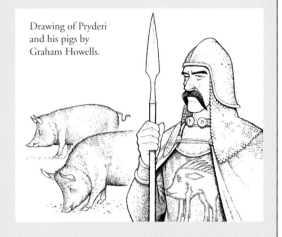

Drawing of Pryderi and his pigs by Graham Howells.

Ceridwen, the goddess of inspiration and keeper of a magic cauldron. When Henwen was about to bring forth her litter, she went to Penrhyn Awstin in Cornwall, where she entered the sea and swam to land at Aber Taroqi in Gwent Is-Coed. Henwen gave bounty to several areas in Wales, which, according to myth, enabled these regions to prosper.

---

of 22 sows and four boars, and they also keep 15 gilts – young female pigs – as replacements.

It all began by chance about five years ago, shortly after they were married and took over running the farm from Richard's parents. The couple were looking to buy a few pigs to fatten, and heard from a friend about a Welsh Pig breeder who had died, sadly, and whose pigs had been slaughtered. The bloodline had been lost forever. But contact was made with the breeding fraternity and shortly afterwards they had a call from another breeder who was giving up. 'We bought him up lock, stock and barrel,' said Fiona, 'and we'd never go back. We used to have a herd of Welsh Black cattle but we sold them so we could concentrate on our pigs.'

The farm also accommodates Brecknock Cheviot and Torfaen Badger sheep and some Highland cattle, but the pigs are the centre of attention, especially in the show season, when the couple put their best animals into the ring.

'They are gorgeous. We do have a grumpy one, but 95% of them are good-natured and they tend to have fewer problems than other breeds. They don't tend to have leg or feet problems.'

One reason for their rude health may be the accommodation. The pigs have the run of a former cattle shed and a stone yard and can root around in four acres of woodland in autumn and early winter. And there are four paddocks which the sows can dig in turn.

'After they dig up the paddock we will plant it up with something they can eat the following winter,' says Fiona.

The pigs provide the couple with meat, and they also supply the award-winning Bob the Butcher shop in Rhayader. 'We go there every week and he does all the cutting up for us and makes sausages and so on. Without him we would not have grown the business to the size it is now. He needs a regular supply and we can provide consistency and provenance. He has gone elsewhere for his pigs,

Sow and piglets at the National Trust farm at Llanerchaeron.

but always comes back to us – and pays us a premium,' says Julia, who works as an accounts manager for a local company.

They also sell breeding stock. 'We have got the shed space so we can keep more breeding stock than most people – and that side has really taken off in the last twelve months. A lot of people want to keep pigs on their smallholdings, though it's a big jump from fattening a couple of weaners to keeping breeding stock.'

The earliest references to a distinctive Welsh pig come from the 1870s when there was a considerable trade in Welsh and Shropshire pigs into Cheshire for fattening on milk by-products. The pigs were generally a yellow-white, but some were spotted black and white.

Pigs of a similar type were also bred in Cardigan, Pembroke and Carmarthen, but the first moves towards a specific breed society began in South Wales with the formation of the Old Glamorgan Pig Society in 1918. Volume One of the herd-book was published in 1919.

A meeting at Carmarthen in 1920 led to the foundation of the Welsh Pig Society in west Wales, and its first herd-book was published in 1922, the same year that the two breed societies amalgamated to become the Welsh Pig Society with offices at Shire Hall, Carmarthen.

After the Second World War, the Welsh breed prospered greatly, as increasing supplies of animal feed led to a dramatic increase in the national pig herd. The number of government licenses issued for Welsh boars increased from 41 in 1949 to 1,363 in 1954, making the Welsh the number three sire breed in Great Britain behind the Large White and Landrace.

In 1952 the Welsh breed joined the six other pedigree breeds that were already part of the National Pig Breeders Association – now known as the British Pig Association. The first NPBA herd book containing entries for Welsh Pigs was published in 1953.

Troedyraur

The Evans family at Troedyraur farm in Brongest, Ceredigion, has the oldest herd of pedigree Welsh pigs in the world. The sow pictured below, which was bred out of the James family, is pictured after their win at the Royal Welsh Show in 2005.

Troedyraur pigs out on grass in 1959.

ACKNOWLEDGEMENTS

The author and publishers gratefully acknowledge the following sources of images:

p.3: Welsh Corgi, cigarette card issued by Gallaher Ltd.; p.4-5: Talymignedd Isaf by permission of Arwel and Sioned Jones and family; p.6: beef at Y Polyn, Simon Wright; p.7: Tŷ Llwyd herd by permission of John James; p.8-10: White Park cattle, National Trust, Dinefwr; Welsh Blacks (below), Colin and Jacqui Rouse; p.11: Castell Dinefwr, Ken Day, taken from *Beloved Tywi* (Gomer 2006); p.12: Welsh Harlequin drake, Greenway Poultry, Rosebush; p.12-14: Welsh Harlequin ducks, Colin and Jaquie Rouse; p.13: painting of Hywel Dda, National Library of Wales; p.15: Welsh Magpie (top), Mike and Chris Ashton; Chewy Magooey ('Tuxedo Chewy'); p.16-18: Brecon Buff geese, Colin and Jaquie Rouse; p.19: drawing of drover's geese, Brett Breckon, taken from *A Christmas Collection from Wales*, Chris S Stephens (Gomer 2008); p.20-22: Derwen stud cobs by permission of Ifor and Myfanwy Lloyd; p.24 Welsh cob (top) G.H. Parsons; p.24-27: Welsh ponies and family photographs, Dr Wynne Davies; p.28-31: Llanwenog sheep, Elfyn and Sharon Morgan and family; p.32: Welsh Mountain ram, Moss Jones WAOS Ltd.; p.33: Balwen sheep, Jamie Wright, taken from *The Wright Taste*, Simon Wright (Gomer 2008); p.34-35, Welsh Mule, Moss Jones WAOS Ltd.; p.36-39: Welsh pigs, National Trust, Llanerchaeron; p.39: Welsh pigs at Troedyraur by permission of the Evans family, Troedyraur, Brongest (welshbloodstock.co.uk)

Front cover photographs: Magpie ducks, Mike and Chris Ashton; Welsh pig, National Trust, Llanerchaeron; White Park, National Trust, Dinefwr

Back cover images: Welsh Mountain lamb, painting by Keith Bowen taken from *Snowdon Shepherd* (Gomer 2009); Welsh pig, National Trust, Llanerchaeron; Welsh Harlequin duck, Colin and Jaquie Rouse

Inside back cover: White Park, National Trust, Dinefwr

It has not been possible to trace the owner of copyright in every case. The publishers apologise for any omission and will be pleased to remedy any oversight when re-printing.